CW00430686

[During Holy Week] a woman entered
very expensive oils on Jesus' head. T
were infuriated with her for this wast~ ~· ~~uney. But Jesus said,
"Let her alone. Why do you criticize her? She has done me a kindness."
Mark 14:3–9

REFLECTION

Acts of generosity, free-will offerings to the needy, stockings full of eyes-
exciting gifts, packages bulging with "just
what I wanted"—these acts of thoughtfulness
reveal the spirit of Christmas. Because God
was so kind as to send us the very best of
gifts, we copycat God's loving kindness by
kindness of our own. The unnamed woman
of Mark's gospel somehow sensed that Jesus'
dignity demanded a special gesture of
respect. She was most generous; then Jesus
returned the favor. Our Lord reserved a place in heaven for her . . . and,
as an "extra," he stipulated that her gift-giving shall never be forgotten.

> **ADVENT PROMISE**
>
> IF YOU ARE GENER-
> OUS TO OTHERS,
> JESUS WILL COME
> TO YOU.

THE GENEROUS WOMAN SPEAKS TO YOU

"Blessed are you, and worthy of God's praise, for all your acts of generosity this year. My gift to Jesus was instinctive. I loved him and trusted his love for me. So I had to demonstrate this love, somehow.
Bystanders, even the apostles, criticized me for overdoing it. There may
be people in your life who will criticize you for the same reasons: 'You
are too generous,' they will say; or 'You are overdoing it with time and
money for so-and-so!' Never mind them. By your good instincts, your
initiatives with love, you are learning about God's 'Bethlehem initiative'
with you."

PRAYER

Jesus, bless me with double blessings for the kindness I am prepared to
give to others. Bless me once by approving of my generosity, just as you
blessed the woman who was so kind to you. And bless me in a second
way, as well: by the love I give to others, help me to know better the
Christmas love I receive from you. Amen.

WEDNESDAY OF THE FIRST WEEK

Hearing that Jesus was passing by, the blind beggar, Bartimaeus, cried out, "Jesus, have compassion on me!" Many people scolded him to make him keep quiet. But he only called louder for help. "I want to see," he said to Jesus. And he received his sight.

Mark 10:46–52

REFLECTION

Yesterday, the woman who gave Jesus a generous gift was severely criticized. Today, a crowd of people sternly rebuked Bartimaeus for "wasting the Lord's time!" Maybe the same thing is happening to you this Christmas season. Some people may be criticizing you for your kindness to others; some may start scolding you for the way you (according to them) "waste precious time helping so-and-so" or "spend too long in your prayers or other pursuits that do not involve me." Never mind. If love has a part and a purpose in whatever you're doing, then what you are doing is already blessed.

> ADVENT PROMISE
>
> IF YOU FAITHFULLY PRAY FOR WHAT YOU NEED, JESUS WILL COME TO YOU.

BARTIMAEUS SPEAKS TO YOU

"Blessed are you when you ask Jesus to help you in your needs. Don't be overly concerned about those who scold you for inconveniencing them. You know in your heart that your kindness to others and your appeals to God are Christ-connected. You are making a good Advent by spending time in such other-reaching ways. You are blessed because you have already embodied the healing hospitality of Jesus."

PRAYER

Jesus, help me to do the right things this Advent. There are so many ways to spend my time, so many people asking for my help that it's difficult to make the right choices. Don't let me neglect to pray for my own needs; don't let me neglect the needs of others. Then once I have set my course and my choices, don't let rebukers ruin me with doubts. Amen.

THURSDAY OF THE FIRST WEEK

[Jesus went up to pagan territory with his disciples. He wanted no one to recognize him, but he could not escape notice. A woman begged him to cure her daughter . . . and he told her,] "It is not right to take the food of children and throw it to the dogs." She replied, "Please, Lord, even the dogs under the table eat the family's leavings." Jesus said, "For such a reply, your faith has saved you . . . your request has been answered."   Mark 7:24–30

REFLECTION

Centuries ago, a woman's patience in the face of adversity allowed the God of all consolations to comfort her. She was a pagan—someone not yet within the reach of Advent. But her daughter was sick, so she cried out loud for help. The apostles were angered by her presence. They didn't want to be noticed. They were looking forward to a few days of rest. Even Jesus seemed to deny her. She did not bristle at this. She did not leave in a huff or scold the apostles for scolding her. She did not return Christ's seemingly ethnic slur with one of her own. She patiently pleaded her cause (with humor) and waited for God's goodness to react to her prayer. Which it did.

> **ADVENT PROMISE**
>
> IF YOUR PRAYERS ARE PERSISTENT AND PATIENT, JESUS WILL COME TO YOU.

THE PALESTINIAN WOMAN SPEAKS TO YOU

"Blessed are you, and you always will be, if you hold off your anger before it leaps to expression. I was tempted to give Jesus a piece of my mind for the way he seemed to shun me. But something made me stop from venting my righteous indignation. Faith saw that Jesus did want to love me and cure my daughter. I'm very happy that I didn't react with bitterness. God's plan of love got to me in its own good time. My story can be yours, if you are patient."

PRAYER

Jesus, my Lord, prevent me from becoming so sensitive to rejection. Let me be willing to wait out your sometimes terribly slow pace. When I am patient with you, maybe I can develop more patience with others this December. And then more patience with myself. And wouldn't that be wonderful! Amen.

FRIDAY OF THE FIRST WEEK

The centurion said to Jesus, "Sir, do not trouble yourself. I am not worthy to have you enter my house . . . I, too, am a man who knows the meaning of an order . . . so just give the word and my servant will be cured."   Luke 7:2–10

REFLECTION

Some people find Jesus by acts of hospitality; others by being humble before God; still others by gift-giving or by intensifying their life of prayer. This soldier, a master sergeant of 100 men, received his Christmas grace because he did his job well. He knew what it meant to take orders and to give them. He was responsible and careful and cooperative. So he applied his work ethic to Jesus'. He reasoned that if he could expect obedience because of his authority, Jesus could expect the same, even from creation. At Jesus' command, the soldier reasoned, even disease will promptly leave the afflicted servant. Jesus praised the man for his reasoning and answered his prayers. But none of it would have happened unless he was a good soldier, a good worker, first of all.

> ADVENT PROMISE
>
> IF YOU ARE RESPONSIBLE ON THE JOB, JESUS WILL COME TO YOU.

THE CENTURION SPEAKS TO YOU

"Be grateful for the power of prayer that can come to you from your ordinary duties in life. Do your work as well as you can. Learn to take orders from your supervisors, teachers, and coaches; and learn to give orders, trusting that others will be as responsible as you are. Then pray, knowing that Jesus in his own time will be as good as you are when you are at your best . . . only he will be better!"

PRAYER

Jesus, let me realize the dignity of my work. I can do things well. I can be trusted. And I can trust others. Both aspects of responsibility make the work succeed. It is the same with you; God spoke, and you were the words he spoke. And you came to us, obedient to your Father's plan of love. Then you spoke your healing words, and all things unhealthy were restored. You have given hope to all creation. You are the heart of Christmas love. Amen.

SATURDAY AND THE SECOND SUNDAY

A herald's voice cried out in the desert, "Make ready the way of the Lord; clear a straight path." . . . All the people of Jerusalem went out to John in great numbers and were baptized by him in the Jordan River as they confessed their sins.   Mark 1:1–8

REFLECTION

Life is full of interruptions. People drop in unexpectedly, phones ring at awkward times, emergencies call us away in the midst of our activities. If we are controlled by great expectations about finishing what we are doing, life invariably causes us much frustration. In the beginning of the gospel story, John the Baptist was doing well. The "desert herald" was making a great impression. Then the authorities threw him in jail. He had to deal with frustration, now that he was placed in the background of the kingdom he began with such a burst of excitement.

> **ADVENT PROMISE**
>
> IF YOU ARE PATIENT WITH FRUSTRATIONS, JESUS WILL COME TO YOU.

JESUS SPEAKS TO YOU

"December is the busiest time of the year. Too much is packed into too little time, and patience is needed more than ever. You will be blessed by my Father and by me if you live with imperfections and the varied expectations of other people. Let the plans you have made be less rigid, and be more sensitive to the plans of those around you. Be like John the Baptist and cooperate with God's agenda. Cultivate flexibility and don't allow yourself to get so upset by what goes wrong."

PRAYER

Jesus, I don't hold my destiny in my own hands. I sometimes think I do, but I don't. Teach me how to trust that you will help me accomplish what I must. Help me to do the best I can without anxiety or harsh words or becoming sullen. Help me to imitate John the Baptist . . . and all the saints who had to change their style of life. Amen.

MONDAY OF THE SECOND WEEK

IMMACULATE CONCEPTION

The angel Gabriel said to Mary, "You shall conceive and bear a son and give him the name Jesus." Mary said, "How can this be?" The angel answered her, "The power from on high will overshadow you." Luke 1:30–35

REFLECTION

ADVENT PROMISE

IF YOU ARE GRATE-
FUL FOR GOD'S
GIFTS, JESUS WILL
COME TO YOU.

Behind God's plan of love was the divine "power of life." That was the original Advent declaration given to Mary. "The power of the most high" would come to Mary and, with her consent, begin the project of salvation for all. Such awesome beginnings had to be foolproof! The dignity of God demanded it. That is why Mary was immaculately conceived. Even though she couldn't have been aware of it, she was created to be the most pure embodiment of the loving plan of God. She was completely gifted for the furtherance of divine compassion. By celebrating this feast day we are really praising God . . . the thoroughness of God's preparations.

MARY SPEAKS TO YOU

"I am grateful for this special celebration of mine. The gift of being born without sin is a gift for me alone. I didn't deserve it. God deserved it! God wanted everything arranged just right because I was to be the mother of the Messiah. You, too, have received a whole assortment of God-given favors at your birth. Without deserving any of them, you received bones that could grow, a brain that could learn, eyes and ears that could function, a home you could feel safe in. If you develop gratitude for the good beginning God has given you, that sense of gratitude is itself the first step of Advent. Thankfulness is the very best way of welcoming the 'power from on high.'"

PRAYER

Jesus, make me more a giving person and less a griping person. And let me be more spontaneous in giving thanks for the uniqueness I was born with and for all the care that keeps me going. This way, I can thank you for your mother, too. Amen.

TUESDAY OF THE SECOND WEEK

The Pharisees declared, "You do not see any of the Sanhedrin believing in Jesus! Or the Pharisees! Only those who are lost!" Then one of their number, Nicodemus, said, "Since when does our law condemn a man without a hearing?" But they taunted him. . . .

John 7:40–53

REFLECTION

During the first two years of his ministry, Jesus was honored and sought after. Then, when people learned who he really was and what demands he was making, almost everyone snubbed him. Only one of the leaders, Nicodemus, resisted the demand that he should be done away with. Only he reminded the others about the principles of justice and the necessity of hearing both sides of an issue. His courage caused him to be dismissed from the "club," the

> **ADVENT PROMISE**
>
> IF YOU STAND UP FOR JUSTICE, JESUS WILL COME TO YOU.

Sanhedrin. But it earned him Christ's respect . . . and it grew to earn him Christ's friendship and everlasting happiness.

NICODEMUS SPEAKS TO YOU

"Blessed shall you be—forever blessed—if you stick to your principles and demand that justice be done. Gently but forcefully resist those powerful people in your life who threaten you with exclusion if you dare oppose them. You may be treated with contempt by the 'in' group, the 'club' or 'gang.' But Jesus will come to you. The Lord prepares a special Advent for those who witness to the truth courageously."

PRAYER

Please, Jesus, let me be your Nicodemus kind of friend. Let me keep learning about your purposes. Don't allow me to be unduly swayed by people on either side of any argument. Let me be silent, with wisdom's patience, when that is called for. Or let me speak out with unselfish strength, when this is needed. And always, always, let me wait for your coming with joyful hope. Amen.

WEDNESDAY OF THE SECOND WEEK

Martha welcomed Jesus into her home. [Then she got busy preparing a big meal.] Mary seated herself at the feet of Jesus, listening to
his words . . . Jesus said, "Mary has made the better choice . . . let
her remain . . . ." Luke 10:38–42

REFLECTION

In a setting where most people would think Jesus should have praised
Martha for working so hard in the kitchen,
Mary was the one who was praised for notic-
ing that Jesus most of all wanted someone to
listen to him . . . not someone to fuss over
him with a fancy meal. December is a hectic
time. Everyone seems to be pushed too hard,
and have too many things to do. It is tempt-
ing to neglect quiet prayer because we are
being driven on the fast lane of "every-
thing's got to be done by deadlines." Let Mary of Bethany quiet you
down, put up a "Do Not Disturb" sign, and allow you to sit, "listening
to Christ's words."

> ADVENT PROMISE
>
> IF YOU QUIET
> DOWN TO PRAYER,
> JESUS WILL COME
> TO YOU.

MARY OF BETHANY SPEAKS TO YOU

"Blessed shall you be if you let God's Christmas bring love gently into
your consciousness. Never mind all those people who are fussing over
preparations and pulling on you in so many directions. Get unfussed.
Calm down for a good half-hour every day. Be there for Jesus. Now and
then ignore the command: 'Don't just sit there—do something!' Instead,
follow this: 'Don't just do something—sit there.' Sit there and listen to
Christ's words."

PRAYER

Jesus, my Lord, put quiet back into my soul. Let feverish activity sub-
side. I want to be more sensitive to the words you tell me . . . and much
less sensitive to the "hurry ups" I hear. Christmas belongs to you, dear
Lord. And so do I. Amen.

THURSDAY OF THE SECOND WEEK

When Martha heard that Jesus was coming, she went to meet him, while Mary sat at home. Martha said to Jesus, "Lord . . . I am sure that God will give you whatever you ask of him . . . ."

John 11:17–44

REFLECTION

It is interesting that two sisters, so different, were praised on two separate occasions for two very different reasons. Both are Advent instructions for us. In Luke's gospel, yesterday, Mary listened. Good for her. Martha was too busy to listen. Too bad for her. But in today's gospel, Mary was useless. She was fainting away with grief for her lost brother.

> **ADVENT PROMISE**
>
> IF YOU SHOW HOS-PITALITY TO OTH-ERS, JESUS WILL COME TO YOU.

Martha was the model for life on this occasion. She was the "take charge person," showing mastery over her grief and a marvelous conviction of life after death based on her faith in Jesus. Because of who Jesus was, he could raise up the dead body of Lazarus if he wanted to. And so he did. It is good to know that both Martha and Mary—hospitality and prayer—are models for our Advent scene.

MARTHA SPEAKS TO YOU

"I hope you understand that there are many good ways for getting yourself ready to meet Jesus. Indeed, my sister and I speak about the two most essential parts of good preparations. I specialized in welcoming people into our home and in my strong faith in Jesus. I encourage you to do the same. Good deeds can 'set the table,' so to speak, so that God's good deeds may come to you. My sister's quiet prayer describes the other side of Advent's importance. Both kindness and prayer are essential."

PRAYER

Jesus, my Lord, you always loved your friends. You needed their open ears to listen to you and their open house to welcome you. Let me be both for you and for all who are related to me in any way. Please bless my prayerfulness and hospitality. They are the two sure ways to welcome you. Amen.

FRIDAY OF THE SECOND WEEK

Jesus looked up [to a branch of a sycamore tree] and saw Zacchaeus. He said to him, "Hurry down. I want to have supper at your house tonight." Zacchaeus was delighted and said, "I give half of my belongings to the poor." Jesus then said to him, "Salvation has come to this house today."   Luke 19:1–10

REFLECTION

Hospitality, delightful meals shared with friends, generosity to the poor, kindness done for anyone who finds that happiness is elusive—all these are evidences of the "Christmas spirit" that has blessed the world long before Dickens wrote his story or "Santa" St. Nicholas gave dowry gifts to needy girls. Zacchaeus put on a fine dinner for Jesus. He was generous to the poor, and he was also a charming host. He delighted Jesus and was delighted in return. Charm went both ways. He was a man after Jesus' own heart!

> **ADVENT PROMISE**
>
> IF YOU ARE GENEROUS TO THE POOR, JESUS WILL COME TO YOU.

ZACCHAEUS SPEAKS TO YOU

"Blessed shall you be this year—happy with Christ's blessings—if you think little of yourself and more of Jesus and his love for you. Consider how joyful you are when you are generous to those in need and kind to everyone around you. That's the way I found Christmas. My love story started not by the crib, but out on a limb of a sycamore tree. We loved the poor and we liked each other's company. That's why Jesus and I got along so well."

PRAYER

Jesus, my Lord, it's wonderful to read how you enjoyed life in the company of good-hearted people. I want to be one of your friends always. Permit me to join the "Zacchaeus Club." And grant that the exuberance of Christmas love may be with me every day. Amen.

SATURDAY AND THE THIRD SUNDAY

Jesus turned around and noticed [John and Andrew] following him. He asked them, "What are you looking for?" They said, "Teacher, where do you stay?" He answered them, "Come and see." John 1:35–39

The priests and Levites asked John, "Who are you?" He answered, "I am not the Messiah." They questioned him further, "Who then? Elijah? . . . The prophet?" He answered, "I am a voice in the desert, crying out, 'Make straight the way of the Lord.'" John 1:6–8,19–28

REFLECTION
Many people are "personality molders." They want us to fit into their wishes or to form ourselves according to their expectations. That is, many people want to do to us what the priests and Levites wanted to do to John the Baptist. We need a very strong spirit of self-composure to discover who we are and then to reveal this to others. God-rooted confidence will help us be shaped by the spirit of Christ, not molded by any human interest or peer group expectations.

> **ADVENT PROMISE**
>
> IF YOU MAKE ROOM FOR SILENCE IN YOUR HEART, JESUS WILL COME TO YOU.

JESUS SPEAKS TO YOU
"You are blessed by my Father and by me when you prepare for Christmas, as my cousin John did. But you don't have to go out to the desert. Just find a place and time in your ordinary routine where you can make room for quiet prayer. Only then will you understand your true identity and how you are connected to me. Only then will you understand your responsibilities to love."

PRAYER
Jesus, teach me how to quiet down and be patient with myself. Stir up in me a desire for prayer so that I can better understand your love. Don't let me be a foolish follower of group-think. Don't let me be harsh in my opinions about superficial people, either. Just don't let them sway me from doing what I should. Without criticism and without complaints, I want to make myself straight and find my way to you. Amen.

MONDAY OF THE THIRD WEEK

The wise men were overjoyed at seeing the star. Then, entering the house, they found the child Jesus with Mary his mother. They knelt before him and presented him with gifts. . . .   Matthew 2:1–15

REFLECTION

When the Magi first came upon the scene, they were simply following tradition. Their long-standing custom told them not to go empty-handed when meeting royalty. A king deserved a gracious presentation of some kind. But when the time came to perform this ritual, they were astonished by their feelings. They realized how important and how warmly personal were these gifts of gold, frankincense, and myrrh. A flood of joy immediately uplifted them. They were made richer by the gifts they gave. Gift-giving does have that blessed boomerang effect!

> ADVENT PROMISE
>
> IF YOU ARE A JOY-FUL GIVER, JESUS WILL COME TO YOU.

THE MAGI SPEAK TO YOU

"Happy are you—and a full measure of joy will return to you—when you give gifts to those you love this Christmas. You might consider it routine, or boring, or forced on you. You may grumble about the high prices, the frenzy of traffic, the thoughtlessness of shoppers . . . never mind. The delight you can give others is worth it. Make each present a kind of sacrament. That's really what gifts are, signs of love for others, and a hint of the greatest gift that has already been given: Jesus, son of Mary, son of God, the Savior of us all."

PRAYER

Please, Jesus, let me dedicate my Christmas preparations to love and to the delight they will bring. Let my gift-giving be unselfish so that I can more thoroughly experience the giving presence that you are . . . and always will be . . . world without end. Amen.

TUESDAY OF THE THIRD WEEK

A family record of Jesus Christ, son of David . . . Judah was the father of Perez and Zerah, whose mother was Tamar . . . Salmon was the father of Boaz, whose mother was Rahab . . . Boaz was the father of Obed, whose mother was Ruth . . . David was the father of Solomon, whose mother had been the wife of Uriah. . . .

Matthew 1:1–17

REFLECTION

Today's gospel is a long list of Jesus' family tree, 45 names in all. His entrance into human society was well documented. But this is more than a simple genealogy. Four women are introduced. Some called them sinful outcasts, blemishes on the family record. None of them were Jews. Yet Jesus could be proud of his great-great-grandmothers because each of them "took the kingdom of God by storm." They surmounted obstacles and showed initiative. God's plan could not have continued without them.

> **ADVENT PROMISE**
>
> IF YOU DON'T GIVE UP, NO MATTER WHAT, JESUS WILL COME TO YOU.

TAMAR, RAHAB, RUTH, AND BATHSHEBA SPEAK TO YOU

"Blessed are you if you prepare for the coming of Jesus the way we did. Nothing in your life could be as frustrating as the difficulties we faced. And we didn't give up. Read our stories in the Bible. We knew our necessary link with the loving plan of God, and we did something about it. We helped God's plan continue. You can do the same. Blessed are you if you do not get discouraged."

PRAYER

Jesus, help me to be strong, as strong as these ancestors were. Give me the courage to change, when change is called for; and the patience and self-composure to stay with what can't be changed. And, like all the saints, Lord, give me the wisdom that can discover new ways to appreciate your gifts. Amen.

WEDNESDAY OF THE THIRD WEEK

When [Jesus'] mother Mary was engaged to Joseph . . . suddenly the angel of the Lord appeared in a dream and said to him: "Joseph, son of David, have no fear about taking Mary as your wife. It is by the Holy Spirit that she has conceived this child."

Matthew 1:18–24

REFLECTION

Every year, the church celebrates the feast of Joseph the Worker. We should also celebrate the feast of "Joseph the Sleeper" and "Joseph the Non-judger." Both of these titles point out what he did not do. He did not judge Mary. She was pregnant but not by him. A lesser man would have driven her out of his life. Joseph didn't. He puzzled over it, waited, and went to sleep. In his sleep, he dreamed and received God's assurance. Then he did as his dream told him. He responded in faith and accepted the possibilities of God's marvelous plan.

> ADVENT PROMISE
>
> IF YOU COOL YOUR TEMPER AND STOP JUDGING, JESUS WILL COME TO YOU.

JOSEPH SPEAKS TO YOU

"Blessed are you, and worthy of God's praise, if you do not judge others. You are not God. You cannot know the hidden reasons for anyone's behavior; you do not even know the reasons for your own. In the silence of quiet prayer, even in sleep, you can be told about love's plan operating in you. Be open to it. Live your life according to faith, and God will always guide you."

PRAYER

Jesus, my Lord, help me to be more like Joseph who took such good care of you. See to it that I have a peaceful sleep each night, based on a good conscience and healthy work habits. And, especially, let me think of Joseph when I'm tempted to sit in judgment of those who have hurt me. Amen.

THURSDAY OF THE THIRD WEEK

The angel said, "Do not be frightened, Zechariah; your prayer has been heard . . . joy and gladness will be yours."   Luke 1:5–25

REFLECTION

Zechariah was a good person. He prayed daily and never missed the times of public worship. But his faith was not strong enough to admit that God could love him personally. He resisted God's love as soon as it meant that he had to change his understanding of reality. Elizabeth and he were old. God "couldn't" give them a son. He also decided there wasn't much real joy and gladness in his world. When the angel told him, "Your prayer has been heard; joy and gladness will be yours," he couldn't

> **ADVENT PROMISE**
>
> IF YOU PRAY, EVEN WHEN DISCOUR- AGED, JESUS WILL COME TO YOU.

believe this either. He was reprimanded for his lack of faith. Yet, he was also blessed. He was blessed with gladness even when he did not believe it could really happen. Zechariah blesses us with the same warning he was given and with the same assurance he now enjoys.

ZECHARIAH SPEAKS TO YOU

"Blessed are you, this Christmas, if you do as I did, not as I said. Keep praying for joy and gladness, even when life's circumstances tell you it can't happen. Don't give up Mass or public worship just because you're 'not getting anything out of it.' I continued even after all hope for answered prayers was gone. But don't fall away from faith as I did. Nothing is impossible for divine love. And if God wishes to fill you with joy and gladness, this year, then let it happen! Blessed are you if you allow for God's delightfulness."

PRAYER

Jesus, my Lord, give me the blessing given Zechariah, and let me never doubt your love. Help me accept graciously all the joy and gladness you want to give. Stop me from dwelling on feelings of futility, annoyance, or frustration. Help me reclaim my own goodness done for others, and from these sources of remembered kindnesses let me prepare for Christmas. Amen.

FRIDAY OF THE THIRD WEEK

The angel said, "Do not be afraid, Mary. You have found favor with God. You shall conceive and bear a son and give him the name Jesus." Mary replied, "How can this be, since I am a virgin?" The angel answered, "The Holy Spirit will come upon you and the power of the most high will overshadow you." Luke 1:26–38

REFLECTION

God asked Mary to be the mother of the Messiah. She trusted that God knew what was best for her and said yes. How often she must have pondered the angel's words! Would she be a good mother? Would she make the right decisions for her child? She wondered how she could possibly exercise authority over the Word of God made flesh. And yet she wasn't afraid to use her God-given gifts to do what God asked. We, too, are called to be open to God's plan for us and to use our gifts well.

> ADVENT PROMISE
>
> IF YOU LEARN NOT TO BE AFRAID, JESUS WILL COME TO YOU.

MARY SPEAKS TO YOU

"You have received many gifts from God: talents, the capacity for leadership, and opportunities for exercising authority. You can use these gifts for good purposes or for selfish ones. I beg you, use your gifts well. Don't be afraid of your talents and responsibilities. Remember my joy when I showed my child to the shepherds. I was so happy that I had allowed God's power to work through me."

PRAYER

Jesus, my Lord, I ask you, in Mary's name, to help me be open to God's will. Make sure I grow in gratitude for the gifts and talents God has given me. Help me to be like Mary in both my gratitude and goodness. And, like her, let me always trust your Christmas purposes. Amen.

SATURDAY AND THE FOURTH SUNDAY

The angel said to Mary: "The Holy Spirit will come upon you and the power of the Most High will overshadow you; hence, the holy offspring to be born will be called Son of God." Mary said: "I am the servant of the Lord. Let it be done to me as you say."

Luke 1:26–38

REFLECTION

As a rule, we are given, as Mary, only the bare essentials about the future. To prepare for what will come, we are usually told no more than we need to know. Three things: trust God, love others, and be agreeable to what divine providence has in store for you. When Gabriel asked Mary to be the mother of the Messiah, there was no contract signed, no job description, no haggling over terms or going through agents. Mary simply greeted God's plan of love with unwavering trust, pure love.

> **ADVENT PROMISE**
>
> IF YOU TRUST THE FUTURE BECAUSE YOU TRUST IN GOD, JESUS WILL COME TO YOU.

JESUS SPEAKS TO YOU

"My Father will bless you, and so will I, if you learn to trust as my mother did. When it came to God's plan for salvation, she agreed without wavering, without bargaining, without doubting. She didn't make things difficult for my Father. She didn't demand further explanations or assurances. She just said, 'Let it be done to me as you wish.' This must be your attitude as well."

PRAYER

Jesus, my Lord, help me control my worries. I don't know what God has in store for me, but neither did your mother. She learned, through prayer and patience, to go with each day as it came along. She learned how to be your good mother by trusting God and keeping a hopeful heart. Let me let it be done to me —her way. Amen.

MONDAY OF THE FOURTH WEEK

Fear came over all their neighbors, and all these happenings were talked about throughout the entire hill country of Judea. All who heard them pondered them and said, "What will this child become? For indeed the hand of the Lord is upon him."

Luke 1:57–66

REFLECTION

Elizabeth and Zechariah's neighbors are the heroes of this episode. They did the very important pre-Christmas work of pondering. They witnessed the marvelous events surrounding the birth of John the Baptist. Then, lest they forget to be reflective, they "pondered all these happenings in their hearts" to make sure that daily routines did not smother the wonder of their experience. We, too, are invited to ponder the gospel readings on these final days before Christmas.

> **ADVENT PROMISE**
>
> IF YOU PUT "SPIRIT PONDERING" IN YOUR PRAYER, JESUS WILL COME TO YOU.

THE NEIGHBORS SPEAK TO YOU

"Blessed are you and worthy to God's praise if you pray quietly about the true meaning of Christmas. Try to understand how the 'happenings of God' personally involve you. Do not get upset about how little time you have to do so many things. Do what you can without anxiety . . . and don't do what you can't. But whatever you do, don't give up pondering. Never cease to treasure God's love, storing up the meaning of God's Christmas in your heart."

PRAYER

Jesus, my Lord, help me to stop for a while today, to rest from all that I have to do. I am busy—that is true—but I'm not that busy. Teach me how to ponder the events of your beginnings . . . and give me the graciousness to applaud your ever-present welcome. Amen.

TUESDAY OF THE FOURTH WEEK

Zechariah, filled with the Holy Spirit, uttered this prophecy: "Blessed be the Lord the God of Israel because he has visited his people and set them free . . . the tender compassion of our God will shine on those who live in darkness and in the shadow of death."

Luke 1:67–79

REFLECTION

Today's gospel talks about looking forward with hope. Zechariah expresses confidence for people of every generation. "God has visited us," so nothing in the future need ever make us anxious or afraid. "God has remembered the covenant," so we never have to be discouraged or think God doesn't care. God has finished "the work of kindness." Thus, with kindness made fresh for us each Christmas, hope cannot be destroyed.

> ### ADVENT PROMISE
>
> IF YOU ASK MARY AND HER FAMILY TO HELP YOU PRAY, JESUS WILL COME TO YOU.

ZECHARIAH SPEAKS TO YOU

"Blessed are you because you are no longer prisoners of death. You need no longer live in the shadow of fear. For Christ is born to us. God-become-human is covenant for us. He was a child first. He lived, as all people do, knowing he would die. He really died because he was really born. But then his Father raised him up, victorious over death. You have nothing to fear, nothing! God has gifted you forever with the covenant of Christ."

PRAYER

Jesus, my Lord, pour light into my darkness. Even this Christmas Eve, part of me still sits in the shadow of death—part hurt, part shamed, part full of fear. Even so, most of me rejoices. Because of your Spirit, I celebrate the tender compassion of our God. I need you, Jesus, to heal my dark side and to help me thrill to the joy I am preparing for. Amen.

SOLEMNITY OF CHRISTMAS

In the beginning was the Word. The Word was in God and the Word was God. The Word was present to God in the beginning. Without the Word not one thing came into being. The Word became flesh and dwelt among us. And we have seen the Word's glory . . . filled with enduring love.   John 1:1–4

GOD SPEAKS TO THE CHOIRS OF ANGELS, TO HUMANS, TO ALL CREATION

"I like stories. I especially like those folk tales that begin: 'Once upon a time, when wishes really did come true . . .' That's how it always was with me. Before there was a beginning of anything, I wished . . . and the Wish was with me. And the Wish and I—with the Spirit of us both—were very good company, the best of friends.

"And then I wished the world. I didn't have to do it. I wanted to. Exuberance of life has to spill out, somehow. And I looked about and saw that it was good. Then, in the excess of my exuberance, I made humans who had minds and hearts that were blessed with freedom. I wanted them to be like the very Wish of me so they could radiate my goodness, be filled with my enduring love . . . and love me back.

"I took a chance with this. The gift of freedom meant that people could do their own wishing. They often did it wrong. And so I sent my Perfect Wish to them. He was born of Mary and grew up slowly. Then he cured the evils in the world and spoke about me with stories everyone could understand. He died a tragic death . . . and then rose up from death and lives forever. He did all this because I wanted to make sure that no one would live without hope, or grieve without my mercy, or fail to look forward to my pledge of everlasting joy.

"My wish today—and my gift, as well—is that you will understand how Christmas started the very best of all the hope-filled folk tales . . . which says how everyone comes home to me, to the place where wishes really do come true."

CHRISTMAS PRAYER

Good God of Life, your love for me is the greatest of all gifts. This day—and for all days to come—let me never doubt your kindnesses and let me live with some of your exuberance. Amen.

TWENTY-THIRD PUBLICATIONS
P.O. Box 180 • Mystic, CT 06355 • 1-800-321-0411

9 780896 227088